Dinosaurs

RUPERT OLIVER

Illustrated by

BERNARD LONG

HODDER AND STOUGHTON

LONDON SYDNEY AUCKLAND TORONTO

British Library Cataloguing in Publication Data
Oliver, Rupert
   Dinosaurs.
   1. Dinosaurs – Juvenile literature
   I. Title   II. Long, Bernard
   567.9'1   QE862.D5

ISBN 0–340–28609–1

First published 1983.

Copyright © 1983 Martspress Ltd.

Published by Hodder and Stoughton Children's Books,
(a division of Hodder and Stoughton Ltd)
Mill Road, Dunton Green, Sevenoaks, Kent TN13 2YJ.

Printed in Italy   All rights reserved.

Contents

Dinosaurs

When the Earth was Dry

Our Earth is full of the most wonderful plant life. From the steaming rain forests of Brazil to the rolling farmlands of Britain, the world is a green planet. There are a few deserts where it is impossible for plants to grow, but they only cover a fraction of the land. Everywhere else is covered by a rich green carpet. The plant life of the Earth provides food for a wide range of animals.

But the world of two hundred and twenty million years ago was quite different. Much of the land was bare rock or barren desert. It was the period of the Earth's history which scientists have called the Triassic period. During this time, the climate of the Earth was very dry. Therefore, unless a plant grew near to a river or a lake, there was not enough water to sustain its life and it would die.

The animal life of this far-distant time was also quite unlike that of today. There were no birds flying in the air and no furry mammals running around on the ground. The group of animals which dominated the land in those days was that of the reptile.

There were many different reptiles wandering the earth, two of which can be seen in the picture above.

On the left is the plant-eater (or herbi-

vore) *Lystrosaurus*. This strange, bulky animal was of the group of reptiles known as the paramammals. This group had been the most successful family of animals for the previous seventy million years, a very long time indeed.

The *Lystrosaurus* probably spent much of its time in the water where it could eat the plants which grew there.

The *Lystrosaurus* must have been a very ungraceful mover. The thigh bones of this animal projected sideways from its body, just as the legs of a crocodile do today. This made it very difficult for the *Lystrosaurus* to move quickly.

The *Lystrosaurus* lived in or near water because there were no plants for it to eat elsewhere. Most of the earth was barren desert. In the same damp places inhabited by the *Lystrosaurus* lived the earliest frog of which we know.

In this riverside scene from 200 million years ago a *Lystrosaurus* tries to escape a hungry *Euparkeria*. A *Triadobadtrachus* looks on.

Though the paramammals had been so successful, they were soon to be overtaken in the race for survival by another group of reptiles, the Archosaurs.

One of these creatures is chasing the *Lystrosaurus* in our illustration. This Archosaur is known as the *Euparkeria*.

The *Euparkeria* was approximately one metre long – almost the same length as the *Lystrosaurus* – but it was far less bulky than the paramammal.

The *Euparkeria* was a ferocious hunter. It usually moved around on all four legs, but it could run very quickly on its hind legs alone, which were much longer and more powerful than the front

9

legs. This action was very characteristic of the Archosaurs and of their descendants, the mighty dinosaurs.

As the Archosaurs spread over the face of the earth, they pushed the paramammals to the verge of extinction. In fact only a few paramammals survived and these were the smallest members of the group.

These tiny creatures were to survive the rule of the Archosaurs and the dinosaurs. Over millions of years they evolved into true mammals and were able to take over the world when the age of the dinosaurs came to an end.

As time went by the Archosaurs evolved to fill many niches in the environment. That is, they developed in a number of ways in order to take advantage of different methods of survival. Some became plant-eaters, whilst others ate meat.

The First of Many

About twenty million years after the *Lystrosaurus* and the *Euparkeria* roamed the land, the first dinosaurs appeared.

Two of these can be seen here.

The two-legged creature prowling the countryside is known as the *Ornithosuchus*. It was descended from the *Euparkeria*, but was much more advanced.

The *Ornithosuchus* was able to walk on two legs the whole time, unlike the *Euparkeria*, which could only manage this for short dashes. The *Ornithosuchus* could do this because its legs were di-

rectly beneath its body, rather than projecting sideways, as in earlier reptiles.

Along the back and sides of the creature's body were large bony plates. We can only assume that these formed some kind of protection, especially as the plates developed into short, sharp spikes around the neck of the beast.

A curious feature which this predator shared with all other dinosaurs is that it had a large cavity in its skull. No-one is quite sure of the reason for this cavity although some scientists think it was there to contain the jaw muscles or a gland of some kind.

All the early Archosaurs had been meat-eaters, but as time went on, some of the dinosaurs became plant-eaters. One of the first to take this step was the *Thecodontosaurus*. This creature, being only about two metres long, was somewhat smaller than the *Ornithosuchus*.

The *Thecodontosaurus* belonged to the group of dinosaurs known today as the Prosauropod family. This family gained its name because it is thought to have been the ancestor of the mighty Sauropod group which followed it.

The *Thecodontosaurus* itself was only just starting on the long evolutionary trail from meat-eater to plant-eater. Its teeth were very sharp, something more usually seen in meat-eaters. However its teeth were very small compared to the true hunters, so it probably preyed on the small lizards.

The *Thecodontosaurus* was one of the first plant eating dinosaurs. The *Ornithosuchus* was a mighty hunter.

Both of these dinosaurs belonged to a large group of dinosaurs known as the Saurischia group, otherwise called lizard-hipped dinosaurs. Within this group came all the meat-eaters and the mighty Sauropods. The earliest dinosaurs were all Saurischians of one kind or another.

Towards the end of the Triassic Period, a new group of dinosaurs was appearing. This is known as the Ornithischia, or bird-hipped group. All the dinosaurs in this group were plant-eaters. The earliest member of this group which we know of was the *Fabrosaurus*.

It was once thought that all the dinosaurs belonged to one group within which there were the two "families", lizard or bird-hipped. However it is now known that the two "families" were in fact quite separate groups.

The *Fabrosaurus* shows all of the characteristics which separate the two groups from each other. The most noticeable difference is in the structure of the hip. Ornithischians, like the *Fabrosaurus*, had a hip which looked like the hip of a bird, whilst Saurischians, such as the *Thecodontosaurus*, had a hip which resembled that of a lizard.

The *Fabrosaurus* was a small dinosaur. It was only about one metre long. Like many later bird-hipped species it walked on its hind legs and was obviously a fast runner.

Flying Reptiles

In our picture you can see a *Kuehnosaurus*, one of the earliest flying reptiles. The "Wings" of this curious creature

The *Kuehnosaurus* used its extended rib cage to glide from tree to tree. The *Fabrosaurus* was one of the first bird-hipped dinosaurs.

were made up on elongated ribs which supported a flap of skin. The *Kuehnosaurus* would not have been able to fly very well. It could not flap its "wings" in the way birds can. In fact it was probably only able to glide short distances from tree branches to the ground.

As time passed, the climate was changing. We have seen that at the beginning of the Triassic period, the weather was very dry, which meant that plants could only grow near to water. However, the climate was gradually getting wetter and wetter. By the time the Triassic Period came to a close the plant life had spread out until it existed practically everywhere.

Although the types of plants to be seen had not changed very much, the landscape was certainly quite different. Instead of vast stretches of barren land separated by small areas where plants grew, the world was now covered with vegetation. In the lowlands there were many swamps and lakes. Plants such as ferns and cycads, which looked rather like palms, were very common.

This warm, moist, almost tropical climate extended over most of the earth and was to continue for the whole of the next geological period. This great stretch of time is known as the Jurassic Period. It lasted for about fifty-nine million years, from 195 million years ago until 136 million years ago.

The three periods in which the dinosaurs lived, Triassic, Jurassic and Cretaceous, are known as the Mesozoic Era.

Whilst the dinosaurs were taking over the land, another group of reptiles was taking to the air. This was the Pterosaur group. The earliest of the Pterosaurs is known today as the *Dimorphodon macronyx*.

The *Dimorphodon* showed many characteristics of later Pterosaurs, such as hollow bones which helped to reduce weight. However in some ways it was still very primitive, compared with later types of flying reptile. The skull of this one metre long beast was unusually large for its size and must have been very clumsy.

The wing was made up in the same way as in all other Pterosaurs. The fore limbs of the *Dimorphodon* were not particularly unusual except for the fourth finger. This was extremely long. In fact it was longer than the rest of the fore limb. Between this finger and the hind leg was stretched a strong flap of leathery skin. This flap of skin served as a wing. No-one is quite sure if the *Dimorphodon* was able to fly by flapping its wings, as later Pterosaurs were able to do, or whether it simply glided around on the air currents.

The name of this flying reptile was chosen because of the unusual teeth which it possessed. *Dimorphodon* means "two shapes of teeth", which is exactly what it had. In the front of its mouth the *Dimorphodon* had large teeth, while near to the back of the jaw the teeth were much smaller.

The Pterosaurs, as a group, were not dinosaurs. They were descended from the same group of early reptiles as the dinosaurs, but they formed a separate and highly successful group of animals.

We know from fossils of Pterosaurs that their bodies were covered with fur. This is very important because it means that they were warm-blooded. If an animal is said to be warm-blooded we mean that it is able to stay warm by burning up energy inside its body. On the other hand, a cold-blooded animal must rely on the warmth of the sun to heat it.

A warm-blooded animal has several advantages over a cold-blooded animal. For example, a warm-blooded animal can move around faster and longer than a cold-blooded one. It is also able to remain active when the weather is cold. A cold-blooded animal can only move around easily after the sun has warmed up its body.

For many years scientists thought that the dinosaurs were cold-blooded, but recently some scientists have begun to doubt this. They point out that some dinosaurs had long legs which means they would have been able to run very fast. However if the creatures were cold-

blooded, they would not have been able to produce enough energy to run fast. Therefore it is suggested that the dinosaurs must have been warm-blooded in order to use their long legs. Not all the scientists agree with this idea. They point out that warm-blooded animals need much more food that cold-blooded ones. They say that if the dinosaurs were warm-blooded, they would have needed so much food to keep their huge bodies going that they

The *Dimorphodon macronyx*, shown above, was one of the earliest Pterosaurs. Below can be seen some lush Jurassic vegetation.

would have had to eat for twenty-four hours every day, just to stay alive. If the dinosaurs were cold-blooded, on the other hand, they would not have needed so much food and spent only a few hours each day eating.

The Hunters and the Hunted

Here you can see a very famous dinosaur. It is known as the *Stegosaurus*. This plant-eating dinosaur lived during the Jurassic period and was perhaps the strangest member of the Stegosaur family. This family of dinosaurs belonged to the bird-hipped group.

The *Stegosaurus* was about six metres long and may have weighed up to two tonnes. The hind legs of this unusual dinosaur were much longer than the front legs. This would seem to indicate that the ancestors of the *Stegosaurus* were dinosaurs which walked on their hind legs only. But with the course of time, the body of the creature became heavier and bulkier, and it started to walk on all four legs.

The most striking feature of the *Stegosaurus* was the double row of bony plates which lay along its back. These plates were very large, the biggest being approximately a metre across.

There has been a lot of argument about the purpose of these plates. It has been suggested that if there were a lot of veins carrying blood to the plates, then they may have been flapped by the animal to keep it cool, much as a modern elephant may use its large ears.

The most popular suggestion is that the plates provided some form of defence for this peaceful plant-eater. There are, however, two rather serious drawbacks to this theory. The first is that if the plates stuck up in the air, they would have provided no protection at all for the sides of the animal. So the *Stegosaurus* would have made an easy meal for any hunter which attacked it from the side.

The *Stegosaurus* lived during the Jurassic Period and belonged to the group known as Plated Dinosaurs

To solve this dilemma, some scientists have suggested that the plates stuck out sideways so as to protect the flanks of the animal.

The second weakness of the theory that the plates were protective is more difficult to explain. It is that the plates were not attached to the skeleton. This means that any attacker could easily have bent them to one side. A suggestion that may solve all these problems is that the plates usually lay flat, but if the *Stegosaurus* sensed any danger, or saw a meat-eater approaching, it would suddenly raise the plates into the vertical position. This sudden change in the appearance of the *Stegosaurus* might have been enough to discourage the attack, or by surprising the attacker, at least have given the *Stegosaurus* time to escape.

One thing which we do know about

the *Stegosaurus* is that it was a very slow mover. This can be deduced from the fossil skeletons of the creature. It has been found that the thigh bone was about twice as long as the shin bone. This indicates that the *Stegosaurus* walked very slowly.

Another bird-hipped dinosaur from the Jurassic period was the *Camptosaurus*. In the picture above a *Camptosaurus* is being chased by a great hunter

The *Camptosaurus*, right, was amongst the favourite prey of the mighty *Allosaurus*, left.

of the Jurassic period, the *Allosaurus*.

Unlike the *Stegosaurus*, the *Camptosaurus* walked on its two hind legs. The name *Camptosaurus* means "bent lizard" and refers to the thigh bones of this five metre long herbivore. These bones were curved, a feature rather unusual in dinosaurs.

The bird-hipped dinosaurs remain the only group of reptiles that ever developed cheeks. This was important, for the cheeks allowed the bird-hipped dinosaurs to chew their food much more effectively and to take larger mouthfuls. This rendered the bird-hipped group very successful as plant-eaters.

The greatest hunter of the time was the *Allosaurus*. This eleven metre long hunter was a lizard-hipped dinosaur and may have been descended from the *Ornithosuchus* of the Triassic period.

Like all the meat-eaters from this time, its head was large in comparison with its body. Normally this would have made the head heavy and cumbersome which would have been a disadvantage when hunting. But the *Allosaurus* and other similar dinosaurs had very light skulls even though they were so large. They were light because the skull bones were very thin indeed. Not only this, but there were large holes in the skull walls.

However the lightness of the skull and the structure of the teeth make it unlikely that the *Allosaurus* used its strong jaws for hunting.

It is much more probable that the *Allosaurus* used its powerful hind legs to bring down its prey. Each hind leg ended in a wicked-looking foot. Attached to these feet were four toes. One was rather small and pointed backwards, but the other three pointed forwards and ended in long sharp claws. A single blow from one of these formidable weapons must have been powerful enough to bring down other large dinosaurs such as the *Camptosaurus*.

Life in the Ancient Seas

On the opposite page can be seen one of the Plesiosaurs, a very important group during the Jurassic period. This particu-lar Plesiosaur is known as the *Cryptocleidus oxoniensis*. Its fossils have been found near Oxford, England. The fossils of more than ninety species of Plesiosaur have been found. So they must have been very successful in the seas of 150 million years ago.

The Plesiosaurs used their strong flippers to swim through the water. These flippers evolved from the legs of the Plesiosaurs' ancestors. Originally the ancestors of the Plesiosaurs had been reptiles which lived on the shore many millions of years earlier. These land-based reptiles evolved into the aquatic Plesiosaurs, long-necked and superbly adapted for a life of hunting fish in surface waters of the seas.

Though the Plesiosaurs were giant reptiles and lived during the time of the dinosaurs, they were not dinosaurs. As far as we know, not a single dinosaur ever took to a life in the seas. Even so, the Plesiosaurs were not the only reptiles to thrive in the Jurassic oceans.

The crocodiles, which first evolved in the late Triassic, were an important group of sea reptiles during the Jurassic. The group as a whole is known as the *Thalattosuchia* group and contained several families within it. One of these families was the *Metriorhynchus*.

In the picture overleaf you can see a *Metriorhynchus*. Members of this family sometimes grew to seven metres long. The *Metriorhynchus* was the best adapted of all the marine crocodiles. It had a tail with which to propel its body through the water. The limbs of this sea crocodile were quite different from the legs of the land crocodiles. In the

150 million years ago the seas were full of strange reptiles, such as the *Cryptocleidus oxoniensis*, seen here.

Metriorhynchus they took the form of small flippers which were probably used for steering rather than for pushing the creature through the water.

Most other types of sea crocodile had some form of armour covering their bodies, but this was absent in the *Metriorhynchus*. This meant that the creature was much faster and more manoeuvrable than its heavier built relatives.

The *Metriorhynchus* hunted fish in the Jurassic seas and formidable predator it must have been, with its turn of speed and powerful jaws. The teeth of the creature were well suited to a life of hunting fish. All of its teeth were razor sharp, but in its upper jaw it had three pairs of very large teeth with which to grasp its prey.

Like the Plesiosaurs and other sea-going reptiles, the *Metriorhynchus* had a curious habit of swallowing stones. The

stones were very useful to the crocodile because they remained in the stomach and ground up large pieces of food into smaller lumps ready for digestion. These stones are called gastroliths and they were absolutely necessary for creatures such as the sea crocodiles which bolted down lumps of food without chewing.

A problem which the *Metriorhynchus* shared with all other marine reptiles was that it breathed air. Because of this, it had to come to the surface at intervals to breathe. If the creature had had to raise the whole of its head out of the water to breathe, it would have been wasting a lot of energy. This problem was solved for the *Metriorhynchus* by virtue of the fact that its nostrils were on the tip of its snout. This meant that it only had to raise a small part of its heavy skull clear of the water, thus making breathing much easier.

Despite all these useful adaptations for life in the open sea, the *Metriorhynchus* became extinct soon after the close

Crocodiles have not always been sluggish riverside creatures. The *Metriorhynchus* was an agile hunter in the seas.

of the Jurassic period. There are no sea crocodiles to be seen in the world today, only their sluggish land based cousins.

Giants of the Jurassic

Whilst the Plesiosaurs and the sea crocodiles were terrorising the small sea creatures, there lived a group of dinosaurs about which there has been more misunderstanding than any other.

This was the Sauropod group, sometimes known as the Brontosaurs or Thunder-lizards. This group included the great *Diplodocus carnegii* and the *Apatosaurus*, both of which can be seen in the illustration over the page.

Overleaf can be seen two hugh Sauropod dinosaurs, the *Apatosaurus*, right, and the *Diplodocus*, left, which was thirty metres long.

23

The Brontosaurs were lizard-hipped dinosaurs, the only members of the group to take to eating plants with much success. It is possible that they were descended from the Prosauropods, though this is not known for certain. The Sauropods walked on four legs, but it is thought that their ancestors may have stood on their hind legs only. This is because the hind legs of the Sauropods were rather longer than their front legs.

For many years scientists also thought that these huge creatures (the *Diplodocus* could grow to a huge thirty metres long) lived in swamps and spent much of their time under water.

There were many reasons for this supposition. One was that such huge creatures could not possibly have supported themselves on land. They must have needed the support of the water to keep them half afloat and take some of the weight from their legs. Another reason for the theory that these huge beasts lived in swamps was that the teeth in the small head were weak and peg-like. Such teeth, it was believed, could only have chewed soft water plants. Finally some fossilised tracks were found of a Sauropod which had been swimming along using its front legs to push on the muddy bottom of a lake. This was seen as proof that these creatures lived in the water.

But recently this idea has been questioned. It is now thought that the mighty Sauropods may have lived on dry land. It has been found that the legs of these creatures were quite able to support their weight. In fact the massive legs could have taken a load of three times the weight of the creature itself.

The teeth of these huge beasts were also found to be not what they had seemed. It is true that they were simple and peg-shaped, but they were not weak. The jaws of the *Diplodocus* and other Sauropods were full of teeth which were quite capable of dealing with the tough plant food which a land-living animal would have had to eat.

It would therefore seem that the traditional idea of the giant Sauropods spending their time in swamps could well be wrong. Instead we should picture these impressive dinosaurs wandering around the Jurassic landscape, browsing on vegetation from the tops of trees which other creatures could not reach.

The *Diplodocus carnegii* was the longest of the Sauropods. It was twenty-eight metres long. The name *Diplodocus* means "double-beamed". This refers to the incredibly long neck and tail to be found on either end of its body. The *carnegii* part of the animal's name comes from the name of the gentleman who paid for the bones to be excavated – Andrew Carnegie. Mr Carnegie was one of the greatest fossil collectors of all time.

The *Apatosaurus* used to be known as the *Brontosaurus*, but it was found that the bones of the *Brontosaurus* were the same as those of the *Apatosaurus*. Because of this a name had to be found to sort out the confusion. As the fossils of the *Apatosaurus* had been found first, it was decided to call the creature by this name.

The *Apatosaurus* was shorter than the *Diplodocus* but was much heavier. It was heavier because of its sturdier build.

The front legs of nearly all the Sauropods were shorter than their hind legs. But the *Brachiosaurus brancai* had longer fore legs. The name *Brachiosaurus* means "arm-lizard" and refers to this particular characteristic of the creature.

Another giant dinosaur was the *Brachiosaurus brancai* from North America.

The Sauropods were at the height of their success during the Jurassic period. At this time, they dominated the role of plant-eater, but soon the bird-hipped dinosaurs were to become supreme. During the next great period in the history of the world, known as the Cretaceous period, the Sauropods were to decrease in number, though a few survived up to the end of the age of the dinosaurs. However this decline in their fortunes was still a long way in the future. For some millions of years to come the Sauropods were to remain the main plant-eating group of dinosaurs. And as such, they were the main prey of the large carnivorous dinosaurs of the period.

Predators, Large and Small

We have already seen one formidable hunter, the *Allosaurus* (see page 19). There were many species of these meat-eaters, but by far the strangest was the *Ceratosaurus*. This dinosaur was rather smaller than the *Allosaurus*, being about six metres long. But it is not this which made it such an unusual beast. On the tip of its snout the *Ceratosaurus* had a bony horn. It is this horn which marks it out from the other meat-eating dinosaurs. Many plant-eaters have horns to protect themselves from meat eaters, but quite why this meat-eater needed a horn is unclear. But if the horn does not fit neatly into the usual scheme of things, it is easier to discern the advantage of having those strange bony growths over the eyes of the *Ceratosaurus*. They would have given some protection to the eyes during fights.

Creatures such as the *Allosaurus* and the *Ceratosaurus* were the most powerful hunters of the Jurassic period. But not all of the dinosaur meat-eaters were so large. There was a whole family of smaller hunters known today as the Coelurosaurs. The Coelurosaurs were able to run very fast and had strong hands which could hold things, unlike the talons of the larger hunters.

The smallest dinosaur of all was a Coelurosaur and it lived 150 million years ago during the Jurassic period. This tiny dinosaur is known to scientists

The *Ceratosaurus* surveys the countryside while a *Tricondon*, an early mammal, is chased by a *Compsognathus*, the smallest dinosaur yet found.

The diagram above shows a comparison between a bird's wing and the wing of a Pterosaur.

as the *Compsognathus*. It was only sixty centimetres long, about the size of a chicken.

The *Compsognathus* was able to run very fast, using its long legs. This must have been very useful because it lived by hunting small lizards and perhaps some of the larger insects.

The eight centimetre long head of this dinosaur was at the end of a long and very flexible neck and this would have been useful too, enabling the *Compsognathus* to move its head around looking for food.

There were many different species of Coelurosaur. Some of them were much bigger than the *Compsognathus*, but not so big as the mighty *Allosaurus*. They were a successful family and survived up to the end of the age of the dinosaurs.

The Feathered Reptile

One hundred and fifty million years ago, at the same time as the *Compsognathus* was running about, the first

The first bird for which fossils have been found is the *Archaeopteryx*, left, from the Jurassic Period.

bird was flapping its wings. This bird is known as the *Archaeopteryx*. It was a very strange looking creature, being just as much a reptile as a bird.

The *Archaeopteryx* was not very big. In fact it was only about the size of a pheasant. But it was very important in the history of evolution. Because it was part bird and part reptile it shows that the birds did descend from the reptiles.

However, although the fossils of this bird have solved the problem of whether or not the birds evolved from the reptiles, they have raised several other questions which have not yet been completely answered.

Once scientists had decided that the birds had descended from the reptiles, the next question was – which reptile?

The best answer seems to be the Coelurosaurs. There are many similarities between the skeletons of the *Archaeopteryx* and the skeletons of the Coelurosaurs. Not only was the general shape of the body very similar, but the structure of the bones in the neck and back was almost identical. However

31

there are two differences between the skeletons of the *Archaeopteryx* and those of the Coelurosaurs – the arm of the *Archaeopteryx* was longer, to form a wing, and the hips were of different types. So perhaps the case for the Coelurosaur is not quite water-tight.

Another problem connected with thinking that the *Archaeopteryx* descended from the Coelurosaur is – why would the Coelurosaur want to fly?

One suggestion is that it did not really intend to fly, but developed long arms fringed with feathers to trap or scoop up its small prey. Only after it had evolved wing-like limbs for this purpose did it start to fly – possibly just taking off when it made a long run on the ground.

A second suggestion, and one which is more popular with scientists, is that the *Archaeopteryx* developed and used its wings to glide from branch to branch in the forest. It is thought that the Coelurosaur chased small mammals or reptiles in the trees. If this were so, then being able to glide would have been an advantage and it would have been beneficial for the Coelurosaur to develop gliding wings and become the *Archaeopteryx*.

One thing we know for certain about the *Archaeopteryx* is that it could not fly very well. The muscles attached to the wings were weak. There was no question of flapping the wings very hard. So probably it is right to believe that the *Archaeopteryx* never did much more than glide around.

The *Rhamphorhynchus* was a more advanced form of Pterosaur than the *Dimorphodon* (page 15). The *Kentrosaurus* on the left of the picture, was related to the *Stegosaurus* (page 17).

Another strong reminder of this first bird's reptilian ancestry is its bony tail. This would have been very cumbersome in flight. The tails of present day birds are made up of long feathers.

The *Archaeopteryx* also differed from later birds in the shape of its skull. It clearly had a reptile skull, without the beak of the modern bird. It had jaws full of sharp teeth — a feature soon to be lost in the course of evolution.

African Dinosaurs

Whatever was to come later, in the Jurassic Period, the air belonged to the reptile Pterosaurs. One of these was the *Rhamphorhynchus*, which can be seen in the picture below.

The *Rhamphorhynchus*, whose name means "prow beak", was obviously more advanced than the cumbersome *Dimorphodon* of earlier years. In particular the skull was lighter and more slender. The jaws were narrow and pointed and armed with many sharp teeth. And all of these teeth pointed forwards, a superb arrangement for catching fish. The *Rhamphorhynchus* had a small lozenge shape on the end of its tail and for many years scientists thought that this shape lay horizontally, but now it is believed that it was vertical and used as a rudder to help steer the *Rhamphorhynchus* in flight.

This strange reptile and all the other early Pterosaurs belonged to the group known as the Rhamphorhynchoidea.

This group is characterised by the long bony tail which the later Pterodactyls did not have. It is thought that the

This small dinosaur trying to catch a lizard for his meal is known as the *Ornitholestes*.

members of this group were not very good fliers. A long bony tail is very useful to an animal which spends much of its time gliding. However it is a drawback if the animal flies long distances by flapping its wings. Because of this, we may assume that the *Rhamphorhynchus* spent most of its time gliding.

The dinosaur in the picture with the *Rhamphorhynchus* is known to today's scientists as the *Kentrosaurus*. In the overall shape of its body it resembled a *Stegosaurus*, which can be seen on page 6. Indeed it is considered certain that the *Kentrosaurus* did belong to the same group of dinosaurs as the *Stegosaurus*. This group is known as the Stegosaurs or "plated dinosaurs".

By the time they became extinct the group had been wandering the earth for a very impressive stretch of time – at least forty million years. And not only did the group survive for a very long time, but it was very widespread. The *Stegosaurus* lived in America, whilst the

Kentrosaurus roamed the coastal plains of Africa.

As the *Stegosaurus* presents us with a puzzle so does the *Kentrosaurus*. It had spikes down the back of its four and a half metre length, but their purpose is as unclear as that of the plates of the *Stegosaurus*.

Though the Stegosaurs were to die out at the end of the Jurassic period, many other groups were to survive right up to the end of the dinosaur era. One of these groups was the Coelurosaur group. The Coelurosaurs were small, agile hunters of the lizard-hipped dinosaur family. One of the smallest dinosaurs of all, the *Compsognathus*, which can be seen on page 28, was a Coelurosaur. There were, however, several larger Coelurosaurs, one of these being the *Ornitholestes*. This dinosaur was about two metres long and about one metre tall.

The name *Ornitholestes* actually means the "bird robber" and was chosen because when the creature was first discovered it was thought that the *Ornitholestes* lived by hunting the primitive birds of the time, such as the *Archaeopteryx*. However we now know that there were not enough birds around at the time to provide sufficient food for the *Ornitholestes*. It is surmised today that it lived by hunting insects, small mammals or lizards, as shown opposite.

The *Ornitholestes* was well suited to a hunting lifestyle. Many of its bones were hollow and light, enabling it to get up enough speed to catch its agile and elusive prey.

However being fast is not enough to make a creature a good hunter. The *Ornitholestes* also needed to be able to seize its prey once it had caught up with it. Here the *Ornitholestes'* fore-limbs came into play. Like the fore-limbs of all other Coelurosaurs, those of the *Ornitholestes* were quite useless for walking, but they were very good for grasping. Each hand had two fingers and a thumb with which to grip a victim.

The teeth of this particular Coelurosaur were of a useful needle sharpness, but were rather small. Together with the weakness of the jaw the small size of the teeth indicates that the *Ornitholestes* could not have hunted large prey but small animals such as lizards.

At the end of the Jurassic or the start of the Cretaceous period a group of lizards evolved in such a way that they lost their legs – probably because they took to a burrowing way of life. These lizards became snakes.

The early snakes were similar to the modern boas and pythons in that they were not poisonous.

Though lizards were numerous in the Jurassic period, the dinosaurs remained the main type of reptile on the land. However, life in the prehistoric seas was quite different.

The Fish Lizard

As far as we know the dinosaurs did not take to life in the sea, but this does not mean that there were no large reptiles prowling around the oceans. Indeed we have already met two such creatures, the *Metriorhynchus* and the *Plesiosaurus*. But perhaps the reptiles best adapted to a life in the sea were the Ichthyosaurs. You can see opposite a species of Ichthyosaur, known as the *Nannopterygius entheciodon*.

Unlike the flippers of some other marine reptiles, such as the Plesiosaurs, the flippers of the Ichthyosaurs were not used to power the creature through the water. The tail provided the movement whilst the flippers were used for steering. In later species of Ichthyosaur, such

as the *Nannopterygius entheciodon*, the flippers were very small, but the tail was long and powerful.

The Ichthyosaurs were well developed for a life at sea in a number of ways. Not only did they have fishlike tails to propel themselves through the water, but their whole bodies were fishlike in appearance. It was this shape which earned them the name of Ichthyosaur, which means fish lizard.

The Ichthyosaurs were so well adapted to life in the sea that finally they could not leave it. This created a problem. All reptiles lay eggs and their eggs must be laid on land. The solution found by evolution was very interesting. The mother Ichthyosaur did not lay her eggs anywhere but kept them inside her body. Only after the babies had hatched did they leave the mother's body to swim the oceans.

Both the origin and the end of the Ichthyosaurs are wrapped in mystery. The earliest known Ichthyosaur dates from many millions of years before the *Nannopterygius* swam in the seas. It is known as the *Mixosaurus* and was rather primitive compared with some of the later Ichthyosaurs. In particular it lacked the fish tail. But it was instantly recognisable as an Ichthyosaur with its streamlined body and small fins.

No-one has ever found any fossils of a creature in the process of evolving from a land reptile into an Ichthyosaur. We can only guess that some reptile dwelling near the shore lived by eating fish and that it gradually came to live in the sea. But what sort of reptile this was, we have at present no way of knowing.

Later in the seas of the Cretaceous

The *Nannopterygius* was a very specialised reptile which hunted fish in the Jurassic seas.

period, the Ichthyosaurs became much rarer until they finally became extinct long before any of the other great sea reptiles.

Why the Plesiosaurs should have survived when the superbly adapted Ichthyosaurs became extinct is one of the mysteries of the age of the dinosaurs.

A Gentle Giant

Although the close of the Jurassic and the start of the Cretaceous Periods, about 136 million years ago, heralded the decline of the Ichthyosaurs, quite the opposite was true of the dinosaurs.

The Cretaceous Period is often referred to as the Golden Age of the Dinosaurs, because there were so many types and they were so successful. Yet, when the Cretaceous Period drew to a close, not a single dinosaur was left alive.

However, 130 million years ago, the dinosaurs still ruled the world.

A very well known and common dinosaur of this time was the *Iguanodon*. The *Iguanodon* was a huge plant-eater, from the bird-hipped group of dinosaurs. It stood about five metres tall when it was upright.

The short front legs of this giant were, like those of many other dinosaurs, quite useless for walking, but they were good at holding foliage while the *Iguanodon* bit off the succulent leaves it liked to eat. The thumb on each of the *Iguanodon*'s hands consisted of a sharp spike, which projected at an angle from the other fingers. This spike could have been used by the *Iguanodon* to defend itself, or to dig up roots for food.

The *Iguanodon* is famous because it was the first dinosaur to be discovered by scientists.

During the Cretaceous Period giant plant eaters, such as the *Iguanodon*, roamed the Earth.

More than 150 years ago, a lady was out for a walk in Southern England, when she came across some fossilised teeth and bones. Carefully she showed them to her husband, Dr. Mantell. He realised that the teeth did not belong to any animal alive at the time.

Because of the size of the teeth, it was obvious that the creature to whom they had belonged had been very large indeed. The strange teeth were the same shape as the teeth of a small reptile called the Iguana. For this reason Dr. Mantell named his find *Iguanodon*, which means "Iguana-tooth".

For many years it was thought that the *Iguanodon* looked like a giant Iguana, walking on four legs. But then several complete skeletons were found in Belgium and these enabled scientists to picture the true appearance of the creature, that is, walking on its hind legs and using its front 'legs' for grasping.

Some Unusual Dinosaurs

Over the page you can see one of the most ferocious of the hunter dinosaurs, the *Deinonychus*. It was related to the

Overleaf can be seen a *Deinonychus* attacking a *Psittacosaurus*.

Below is a diagram of the foot of a *Deinonychus* showing its fearsome claw.

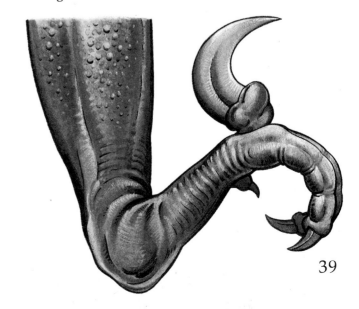

Coelurosaurs, but far more dangerous.

This beast was not the largest of the meat-eating dinosaurs. It was only about three metres long, but it had a unique and formidable asset. One toe on each foot carried a huge, sharp claw at least twelve centimetres long. This curved blade must have been used as a weapon, for the *Deinonychus* held it high off the ground and used its other two toes for walking.

Like the Coelurosaurs, the dinosaur was built for speed and agile movement. But it was not content to live off small reptiles or mammals. It has a large, strong skull, more like that of the *Allosaurus* than of the *Ornitholestes*. This indicates that the *Deinonychus* could tear meat from a carcass rather than be content and swallowing the little prey.

In our illustration you can see a *Deinonychus* attacking a small herbivorous dinosaur, a *Psittacosaurus.*

From the fossil evidence scientists have a fair idea of how the *Deinonychus* hunted its prey. Once it had spotted a likely victim, it would use its exceptional turn of speed to catch up with the hapless plant-eater. It would then fell its victim with a pouncing movement.

The *Psittacosaurus* being attacked by the *Deinonychus* in our illustration was a member of the bird-hipped group of dinosaurs and was very important. Scientists think that this two and a half metre long creature may have been the ancestor of the Ceratopsian family of dinosaurs. This family was prominent during the later part of the Cretaceous period. On the cover of this book you can see a *Triceratops*, a member of this family. There were dozens of species of Ceratopsians, some of which we shall meet later in this book.

The *Psittacosaurus* itself is something of a problem. How could such a clumsy, slow-moving animal possibly survive competition from other plant-eaters and also the attack of predators? The answer to this seemingly difficult problem may be found in its teeth.

During the Cretaceous period, the plant life of the world changed drastically. It was then that the first flowering plants appeared. Today flowering plants account for about three quarters of all the plant species, including trees, grass, bushes and many, many others. None of these was to be seen before the Cretaceous period. It is a characteristic of flowering plants that they grow more quickly than non-flowering plants, therefore when these new plants took over the world there was a lot more food for the plant-eating dinosaurs to eat. This was to lead to a dramatic increase in the numbers of different types of dinosaurs.

These new plants were much tougher to eat than the older plants had been. But the *Psittacosaurus* had strong jaws and very effective slicing teeth, quite adequate to deal with these tough plants. It also had a large, strong beak to tear off clumps of leaves. This beak gave the creature its name, which means "parrot-reptile".

So it seems that the *Psittacosaurus* had an advantage over other plant-eaters in that its teeth were strong enough to eat the new vegetation. And if in eating it, the *Psittacosaurus* browsed in dense undergrowth, then it would have been hidden from predators – and so it survived.

On the page opposite can be seen two extraordinary beasts, the *Pachycephalosaurus* and the *Quetzalcoatlus.*

The *Pachycephalosaurus* belonged to a small family of dinosaurs known as the bone-heads. These dinosaurs were

The largest known flying reptile was the *Quetzalcoatlus*. It had a wingspan of about 15 metres. In the foreground is a *Pachycephalosaurus*, a type of bonehead.

Fossils of the *Ouranosaurus* have been found in the Sahara Desert.

rather like an ordinary two-legged, bird-hipped dinosaur, except for one extraordinary thing. The bones on the tops of their skulls were incredibly thick – twenty-five centimetres in the case of the *Pachycephalosaurus*.

We do not really know what such an amazing adaptation was for, but scien-tists have speculated that *Pachycephalo-saurus* may have butted their heads when quarrelling over territory, just as bighorn sheep do today. If rival *Pachycephalosaurus* did fight in this way, the large mass of bone on the head would have protected the brain from the crushing impact. It would have needed

44

all the protection it could get, for when two dinosaurs, each four metres long, charged into each other at full speed, the impact much have been enormous.

Because so few complete skeletons of the bone-heads have been found, it may be thought that they were rather rare in their time. But this may not be so. It has been suggested that the bone-heads lived up in the hills and mountains. If this were true, then it would explain the absence of fossils, because creatures which die on high land stand little chance of being fossilised.

The *Quetzalcoatlus* was a flying Pterosaur belonging to the last and most efficient family of Pterosaurs, the Pterodactyls. The Pterodactyls differed from the earlier Pterosaurs in many ways. The first was that they had no tail. This would seem to indicate that they were very good fliers.

They ranged in size from about that of a thrush up to the enormous *Quetzalcoatlus*, which was about fifteen metres from wing tip to wing tip.

Scientists think that this monster of the skies (which is named after an ancient god of the Aztecs) may have lived much as vultures live today. It would have soared high over the prehistoric landscape, keeping a sharp eye open for any bits of food. Once it had spotted something to eat it would have swooped down on its majestic wings and satisfied its hunger.

Another large Pterodactyl can be seen on the contents page of this book. This creature was almost as large as the *Quetzalcoatlus* and is known as the *Pteranodon*. It is thought that the *Pteranodon* flew over the seas and lived by hunting fish. The extraordinary crest on the skull of this reptile was almost certainly used to balance the head.

While the *Pteranodon* was gliding over the oceans using the air currents a most unusual dinosaur was striding across the territory now known as the Sahara Desert. This was the *Ouranosaurus* which can be seen opposite. This large plant-eater was related to the *Iguanodon*, (see page 38) to which it was very similar in structure and life-style. The most striking thing about the *Ouranosaurus* was the large "sail" down its back.

To understand why it needed this tall "sail" we should look at its habitat.

One hundred and ten million years ago, during the lower Cretaceous Period, the Sahara was not a desert, although it was a very hot region. The land was covered in scrubby vegetation on which the *Ouranosaurus* fed. As the *Ouranosaurus* moved from plant to plant it would have become very warm indeed – even warmer if it had to run from a predator.

When an animal over-heats in this way, it is likely to collapse from heat-exhaustion, unless it can cool down. The simplest way for a creature to cool down in a hot climate is to find a patch of shade and lie down for a while.

However, this method would not have been of much use to the *Ouranosaurus*. It would have spent so much time lying down that it would not have had enough time to eat all the food it needed to keep going. Evolution of the "sail" overcame this problem. The "sail" was held upright by strong, slender bone spikes attached to the spine. The skin flap connecting the bone spikes was full of blood vessels which easily dispersed the excess heat from the body of this dinosaur. In this way the *Ouranosaurus* could remain active in the hottest weather.

It was not only the gentle plant-eaters which used this curious adaptation to cope with a hot climate. The hunters used it as well. One of these predators can be seen on page 61. It is called the

The earliest Ceratopsian dinosaur was the *Protoceratops*. Unlike later Ceratopsians it was small and had no horns.

Spinosaurus and its fossils have been found in Egypt.

Dinosaurs with Horns

As time passed, the dinosaurs continued to evolve into many types. One completely new family was the Ceratopsia. The *Psittacosaurus*, which may have been the ancestor of the Ceratopsians, has already been mentioned, but above you can see is a picture of the first certain member of the family. It is known today

as the *Protoceratops* and its fossils have been found in Mongolia.

We know a lot about the *Protoceratops* because many of its fossils have been found. There are even fossils of its eggs. The *Protoceratops* was only about two metres long, but it possessed many features characteristic of its descendants.

The *Protoceratops* was a heavily-built dinosaur which walked on all four legs. This is true of the later and much larger Ceratopsians. But it is the skull of the *Protoceratops* which gives scientists the real clue to its place in the family tree of the Ceratopsians.

In our picture of the *Protoceratops* you can see the large bony frill projecting from the back of the skull and covering the neck. It is often said that this frill protected the neck from the jaws of a hungry attacker. But this is not the only purpose that the frill fulfilled.

The head of the *Protoceratops* took up about a third of its entire length. Some strong muscles were needed to support such a weight. These muscles were attached to the back of the frill and stretched back to the shoulders.

Muscles were also attached to the front of the frill. These worked the jaws and were very powerful. The strong jaw muscles were needed by the *Protoceratops* because it fed on tough plant food.

As well as the frill, the *Protoceratops* also had a sharp pointed bill. This bill together with the frill and certain features of the skeleton mark the *Protoceratops* as the ancestor of the later Ceratopsians.

It is from a remarkable series of finds in Mongolia that we know about the eggs of the dinosaurs. For many years a few eggs were known from the age of the dinosaurs. But no one knew which dinosaur laid them or even if they belonged to a dinosaur at all. Then one day, a clutch of fossilised eggs was found along with the fossils of newly-hatched dinosaurs. They were young *Protoceratops*. At last the scientists had some material on which to work.

It seems that the mother *Protoceratops* dug a hollow in the sand before laying her eggs. She then laid a batch of about twenty eggs arranged in a neat circle. Each of the eggs was about twenty centimetres long and the shell was covered with an odd series of bumps, as were all dinosaur eggs. The eggs were then covered in sand by the mother to keep them warm. For some reason, which we do not know, only a few of the eggs

This nest contains the eggs of a *Protoceratops*. Eggs of this dinosaur became fossilised and have been found by scientists.

47

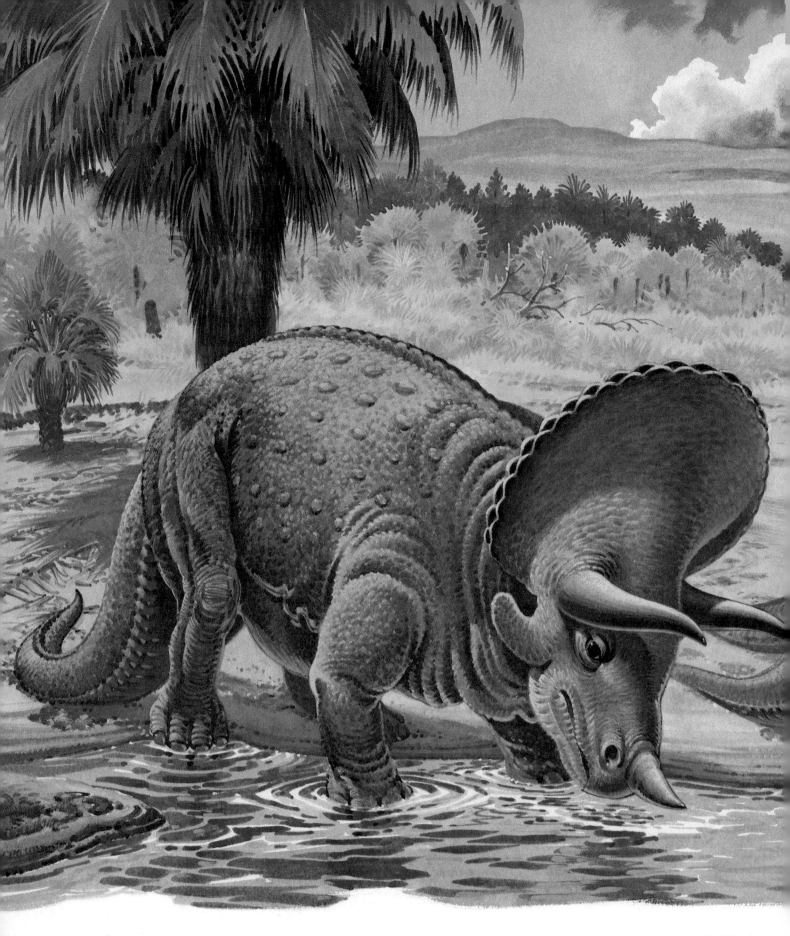

hatched and these babies died alongside the eggs. But this little tragedy of millions of years ago has helped scientists by leaving them much information.

As the Ceratopsian family evolved during the Cretaceous period, they split into two branches, the short-frilled branch and the long-frilled branch. Both branches developed the large horns for which the family is famous.

The largest of the short-frilled branch was the famous *Triceratops*, whose name

48

means "three-horned-face". This monster was about eleven metres long and weighed eight and a half tonnes, much larger than its ancestor, the *Protoceratops*.

The large horns which grew from

The huge *Triceratops* was one of the most common of the Ceratopsians during the Cretaceous Period.

above the eyes of the *Triceratops* were over a metre long. These huge horns

must have saved many a *Triceratops* from the jaws of a hungry hunter. Surely very few predators would have run the risk of getting stabbed by such formidable weapons.

There were several similar species which were very common in North America towards the end of the dinosaur age.

Crested Duckbills

The Hadrosaurs or duck-billed dinosaurs were, perhaps, the most successful family of dinosaurs of all.

The family first evolved during the early part of the Cretaceous period, in Mongolia.

The basic body design was very similar to that of the *Iguanodon* and other large, bird-hipped dinosaurs. The hind legs were mainly used for walking, while the front legs were much smaller. When the dinosaur wished to move on two legs, its long heavy tail would help to balance the body.

The main differences between the Hadrosaurs and the other bird-hipped

Many of the Hadrosaur group of dinosaurs had strange crests on their heads. The *Lambeosaurus*, left, and the *Parasaurolophus*, right, belonged to this group.

plant-eaters were to be found above the shoulders. The jaw bone flared out into a wide flat mouth, rather like a duck's bill. There were no teeth in this front part of the jaw, but the Hadrosaurs made up for this lack at the back of the jaws where there was a great battery of grinding teeth. In one fossil skull, over 2,000 teeth were found.

The most striking thing about the Hadrosaurs, however, was the variety of large crests to be found on their head. These crests were made of bone and most of them were hollow. Two different Hadrosaurs are depicted on this page, the *Parasaurolophus* and the *Lambeosaurus*. Another type of Hadrosaur can be seen on page four. This is known as the *Corythosaurus*. Some scientists think that the crests helped with the sense of smell. As air was inhaled it passed through the crests on the way to the lungs. If the crests were full of scent organs, the Hadrosaurs would have been able to smell a threatening hunter and have had time to escape.

Another suggestion is that the crests were used to produce noises. It is said the hollow crest would have acted like the sound box on a musical instrument to increase the volume of any call the dinosaur may have made. This would have been very useful for passing on warnings of danger.

Many dinosaurs had thick bony armour, such as the *Palaeoscinus*, above.

The lifestyle of the Hadrosaurs is just as much a mystery as the crests. Many features of the Hadrosaurs point towards their living in water. They had broad flattened tails, very useful for swimming and not often found in land-living animals. The fingers of the hadrosaurs were webbed, another adaptation more suited for life in water.

Despite this, many scientists think that the Hadrosaurs were not aquatic dinosaurs at all, but lived on dry land. They point out that the teeth were suited to grinding tough land plants rather than soft waterside plants. Not only this, but some fossil remains included a fossilised stomach. In the stomach were the leaves and twigs of land plants.

But however the Hadrosaurs spent their time, it must have been well spent. By the close of the age of the dinosaurs,

there were far more species of Hadrosaur than of any other group of dinosaur.

Dinosaurs in Armour

The Ceratopsians and the Hadrosaurs were certainly spectacular, but perhaps the most curious of the Cretaceous dinosaurs were the Anklyosaurs. One of these beasts, the *Palaeoscinus*, is depicted above.

The *Palaeoscinus* was built like a living tank. It was about five metres long and weighed well over three tonnes. The feature for which this creature is most famous is its massive armour plating.

Because it was so heavy and ponderous the *Palaeoscinus* could not have run away when danger threatened. It had to rely on its armour. However its underside was completely undefended by armour. This was therefore the weak spot in its defences and had to be protected from attack.

It is thought that when a *Palaeoscinus* sensed a hungry meat-eating dinosaur nearby, it probably squatted down on the ground with its legs tucked under itself. In this position the *Palaeoscinus* was almost immune from attack. Its bony armour completely protected the upper part of its body from the sharp claws and teeth of its no doubt mighty attacker. The only way that the predator could have got at the vulnerable underside of the *Palaeoscinus* would have been to turn it over on to its back. The task of turning over the vast three tonne bulk of a *Palaeoscinus* would have been formidable for even the largest of the Cretaceous hunters.

It is interesting to note that the long rows of spikes which stretched down either side of the *Palaeoscinus* were not used as the *Triceratops* used its spikes. The *Triceratops* would have chased any threatening meat-eater and tried to stab it with its horns. But the *Palaeoscinus* was not equipped to harm its attacker. Those vicious-looking rows of spikes simply made the dinosaur more difficult to overturn.

Other types of armoured dinosaur were just as well protected against attack, so one might expect the family to be very widespread and numerous. However fossils of these heavy creatures are very rare, some species being known only from one incomplete fossil.

The Mighty Killers

The Mesozoic Era is often called the age of the dinosaurs, but they were not the only large reptiles of the time. At the same time when the first dinosaurs were appearing, during the Triassic period, (see page 10), the crocodiles first evolved.

The crocodiles were descended from the same group of reptiles as the dinosaurs, that is the Archosaurs. After millions of years of evolution, the crocodile family produced the mighty *Phobosuchus*, the largest crocodile ever. It was fully sixteen metres long, far larger than any crocodile alive today.

The giant crocodile, *Phobosuchus*, often attacked creatures such as the *Leptoceratops*, when they came to drink.

In our picture the *Phobosuchus* is attacking a *Leptoceratops*. This small dinosaur was about two metres long, the same size as a man. Compared with the *Leptoceratops*, the *Phobosuchus* is simply enormous.

The *Leptoceratops* was a Ceratopsian, the same family as the mighty *Triceratops*, but unlike all other Ceratopsians, the *Leptoceratops* walked on its hind legs. It was a fast, nimble runner, quite unlike its ponderous relations.

It also differed from its relations in that it did not have any horns to defend itself. It must have relied on running from danger. The only thing that connects this oddity to the larger Ceratopsians is its skull. This has the tell-tale neck and frill and similar teeth to those found in the *Triceratops*.

Over the page can be seen the mightiest hunter ever to have prowled the

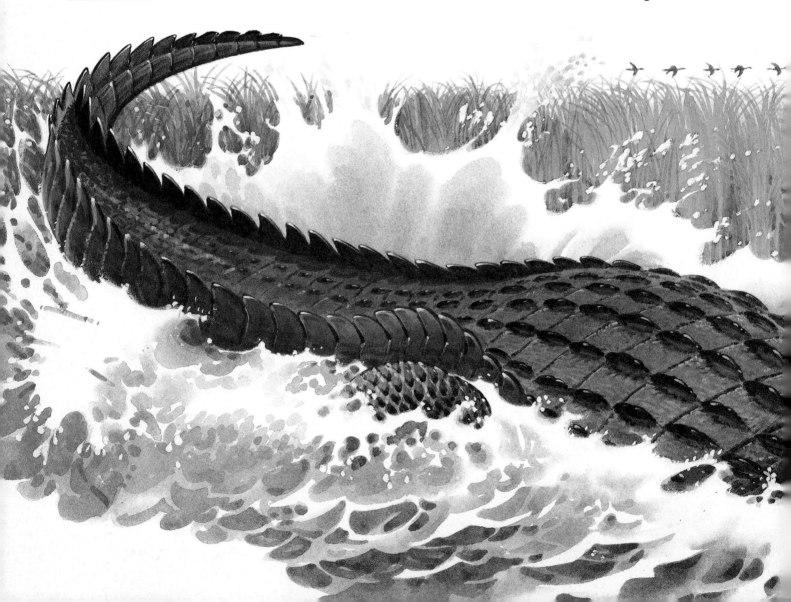

earth, the *Tyrannosaurus Rex*. This huge beast stood about six metres tall and weighed over seven tonnes.

When hunting, the *Tyrannosaurus Rex* would have held its body horizontally. In this position it could have run faster. It is also likely that this beast used the large claws on its hind feet to bring down its prey. Each of these claws was twenty centimetres long.

It is thought that the Hadrosaurs formed the bulk of the *Tyrannosaur's* diet. However occasionally a hungry *Tyrannosaurus* might well have attacked a powerful Ceratopsian. Such an encounter is to be seen overleaf. The *Tyrannosaurus* has tried to catch a young *Torosaurus* by surprise. But it has failed and is now faced by the mother *Torosaurus*, armed with three long horns.

The *Torosaurus* was a long frilled Ceratopsian. In this branch of the

Overleaf shows the dreaded *Tyrannosaurus rex* attacking a group of *Torosaurus* which used their horns to protect themselves.

family, the neck frill grew to quite extraordinary lengths. It extended half way down the back of the *Torosaurus* and its skull measured three metres long.

Against such fearfully armed opposition, even the *Tyrannosaurus* must have stood little chance. Indeed the only way that a *Tyrannosaurus* could have brought down a *Torosaurus* would have been if it could have taken its prey by surprise.

The short spindly arms of the *Tyrannosaurus* seem quite out of place on such a large and powerful monster. However the reason for their existence may be that they helped the *Tyranno-saurus* to stand up. If a *Tyrannosaurus*

had tried to stand simply by straightening its back legs, it would only have pushed its head along the ground. But with the small claws of its forelegs to brace it, the *Tyrannosaurus* could have raised its heavy head off the ground.

Though the small arms may have seemed out of proportion, the same is certainly not true of the jaws of this dinosaur. Each tooth in the mighty jaws was fully nine centimetres long and serrated like a knife. And as well as this the mighty lower jaw was specially hinged so that the *Tyrannosaurus* could take large bites from its prey. This giant creature surely earned its name, which means "King of the Tyrant Lizards".

The Greatest Mystery of All

One of the last dinosaurs was the *Ornithomimus*, a Coelurosaur from the late Cretaceous. Like all Coelurosaurs it was a fast runner and it hunted small creatures. However, it was larger than most other Coelurosaurs, being about four metres long.

The hands of the *Ornithomimus* were very specialised, having long fingers and a strong grip. It is not really certain for what reason the hands were used; perhaps the *Ornithomimus* dug up eggs with them. Or maybe it used its hands to shake bushes in its search for prey.

One certain thing about the *Ornithomimus* is that it became extinct like all the other dinosaurs.

This is one of the greatest mysteries of all time. Why should a successful group of animals die out so suddenly? For well over a hundred million years, the dinosaurs had ruled the earth. No other group of animals came near to challenging them in all that time, but suddenly they were gone.

One thing we do know for certain is that the death of the dinosaurs left a great gap in the animal life of the planet. A gap which was waiting to be filled.

Two other groups of animals took over as the dominant life form. These groups were the birds and the mammals.

In our picture the *Ornithomimus* can be seen with an *Ichthyornis*, an advanced Cretaceous bird.

The birds were to take over from the Pterosaurs, while the mammals came to dominate the land.

The land is now dominated by mammals, not dinosaurs. Like the birds, mammals have never reached the enormous size of their reptilian predecessors, but in some ways they are more successful than the dinosaurs. Mammals have taken to life in the oceans as whales and dolphins, something dinosaurs never did. The mighty Plesiosaurs and the Ichthyosaurs which swam the seas were not dinosaurs as such, though it is probable that they were descended from the same group of reptiles as the dinosaurs. Likewise the Pterosaurs who flew the skies were not dinosaurs, though they too were archosaurian reptiles, but mammals have taken to the air in the form of bats.

The dinosaurs exploited all aspects of life on the land and maintained their superiority in the world for far longer than man or any of his fellow mammals has yet done. These mighty monsters were the pinnacle of the evolution of the reptiles. When we see the fossils in museums we can only stand in awe at the thought of the huge dinosaurs who once dominated this world as their own.

The agile hunter *Ornithomimus* was one of the last of the dinosaurs.

58

Pronunciations

Allosaurus
ALLO-saw-rus

Anklyosaurus
Ank-LEE-o-saw-rus

Apatosaurus
A-PAT-o-saw-rus

Archaeopteryx
Ar-KAY-op-ter-ix

Archosaur
ARK-oh-sawr

Batractosaurus
Ba-TRAK-toe-saw-rus

Brachiosaurus brancai
BRACK-ee-oh-saw-rus BRANK-eye

Brontosaurus
Bron-toh-saw-rus

Camptosaurus
KAMP-toe-saw-rus

Ceratopsian
Sera-TOP-see-an

Ceratosaurus
See-RAT-o-saw-rus

Coelurosaur
SEEL-yoor-o-sawr

Compsognathus
KOMP-sog-NATHE-us

Corythosaurus
Cor-REE-thoh-saw-rus

Cryptocleidus oxoniensis
CRIP-toh-clide-us OX-ohn-ee-en-sis

Deinonychus
DINE-o-NI-kus

Dimorphodon macronyx
Die-MORF-o-don Mak-ron-ix

Diplodocus carnegii
Dip-lo-DOH-cus car-NEE-gee

Euparkeria
U-par-KEER-eeah

Fabrosaurus
FAB-roh-saw-rus

Graculavus
GRAK-u-lave-us

Hadrosaur
Had-roh-sawr

Ichthyornis
IK-thee-or-nis

Ichthyosaur
IK-thee-oh-sawr

Iguanodon
Ig-WAN-o-don

Kentrosaurus
KEN-tro-saw-rus

Kuehnosaurus
CUE-no-saw-rus

Lambeosaurus
LAM-beo-saw-rus

Leptoceratops
LEP-tow-SE-ra-tops

Lystrosaurus
LIS-trow-saw-rus

Metriorhynchus
Metrio-RIN-cus

Mixosaurus
MIX-oh-saw-rus

Nannopterygius entheciodon
Nannop-TER-ee-jus en-thee-SIO-don

Ornitholestes
OR-nith-oh-LES-tees

Ornithomimus
OR-nith-oh-MEE-mus

Ornithosuchia
OR-nith-oh-SOO-cheeah

Pachycephalosaurus
PAK-ee-KEF-alo-saw-rus

Palaeoscinus
PALE-ee-oh-SKINE-us

Parasaurolophus
PA-ra-saw-ro-LO-fus

Phobosuchus
FOBE-oh-SOO-kus

Plesiosaurus
PLEES-io-saw-rus

Prosauropod
Pro-SAW-roh-pod

Protoceratops
Pro-toe-SERRA-tops

Psittacosaurus
SIT-ah-coh-SAW-rus

Pteranodon
Ter-RAN-o-don

Pterosaurus
TER-o-saw-rus

Quetzalcoatlus
KWET-zal-COAT-lus

Rhamphorhynchoidea
RAM-for-RIN-coyd-ee-ah

Rhamphorhynchus
RAM-for-RIN-cus

Sauropod
SAW-roh-pod

Saurosuchia
SAW-roh-soo-cheeah

Spinosaurus
SPINE-oh-saw-rus

Stegosaurus
STEG-oh-saw-rus

Thalattosuchia
Tha-LATTO-soo-cheeah

Thecodontosaurus
THEK-oh-DONT-oh-saw-rus

Torosaurus
TO-roh-saw-rus

Triadobatrachus
Tri-AD-oh-ba-TRAK-us

Triassic
Try-ASS-ik

Triceratops
Try-SERRA-tops

Tyrannosaurus Rex
Ti-RAN-oh-saw-rus REX